Henry VIII

King of England 1509–1547

Written by Ben Hubbard Illustrated by Jennie Poh

DK | Penguin Random House

Author Ben Hubbard
Illustrator Jennie Poh
Subject Consultant Dr. John Cooper
Editor Rea Pikula
Designer Sadie Thomas at LS Design
Senior Editor Marie Greenwood
US Senior Editor Shannon Beatty
Additional Design Charlotte Jennings
Additional Editorial Becca Arlington
Jacket Coordinator Elin Woosnam
Managing Editor Jonathan Melmoth
Managing Art Editor Diane Peyton Jones
Production Editor Gillian Reid
Senior Production Controller Ben Radley
Publisher Francesca Young
Art Director Mabel Chan
Managing Director Sarah Larter

First American Edition, 2024
Published in the United States by DK Publishing,
a division of Penguin Random House LLC
1745 Broadway, 20th Floor, New York, NY 10019

A catalog record for this book
is available from the Library of Congress.
ISBN 978-0-7440-9959-1

DK books are available at special discounts when purchased
in bulk for sales promotions, premiums, fund-raising, or
educational use. For details, contact: DK Publishing Special
Markets, 1745 Broadway, 20th Floor, New York, NY 10019
SpecialSales@dk.com

Printed and bound in China

www.dk.com

Contents

Before Henry

There had been monarchs in England for hundreds of years before Henry VIII took the throne. Each played a part in transforming England into the country Henry ruled over.

The United Kingdom (UK) didn't exist when these ancient rulers were in power. They ruled over the kingdom of England, which then meant England and Wales.

In 1542, Henry also became the King of Ireland.

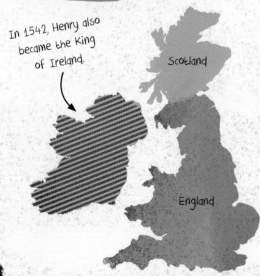

Scotland

England

House of Plantagenet
1154–1485

A royal family called the Plantagenets ruled England and parts of France for more than 300 years. Beginning with Henry II, they produced 14 kings.

House of Lancaster
1399–1461

The House of Lancaster was a branch of the Plantagenets. It gave England three kings: Henry IV, Henry V, and Henry VI. Its symbol was a red rose.

Richard II
1377–1399

Edward III
1327–1377

A true warrior king, Edward III won many wars against France. His children formed the rival houses of York and Lancaster, which would fight over the throne many years later.

Henry IV
1399–1413

Henry V
1413–1422

This monarch gave England a strong identity by making English, and not French, the main language in government. Henry's victory over the French at the Battle of Agincourt was so remarkable that it inspired William Shakespeare to write a play about it.

King Edward III's son, John of Gaunt, was a distant relative of Henry VII. Henry used this as his claim to the throne.

Henry VI
1422–1461

Richard III
1483–1485

Henry VII
1485–1509

After his success at Bosworth Field, Henry Tudor was crowned King Henry VII. His first job was to unite the country, and the warring families.

Wars of the Roses
1455–1485

These were a series of battles that took place between the houses of Lancaster and York. They each believed they had a claim to the English crown, as they were both descended from Edward III.

Edward V
1483

Edward IV
1461–1483

Henry VIII
1509–1547

Born on June 28, 1491, Henry was the second monarch from the House of Tudor. King for almost 38 years, Henry would be remembered as one of England's most influential rulers.

House of York
1399–1461

Another branch of the House of Plantagenet, the House of York produced three English kings: Edward IV, Edward V, and Richard III. Its emblem was a white rose.

Battle of Bosworth Field
1485

The Wars of the Roses ended at the Battle of Bosworth Field when Henry Tudor, from the House of Lancaster, defeated and killed his rival, Richard III, from the House of York.

House of Tudor
1485–1603

When Henry VII became king, the House of Tudor was born. In 1486, Henry married Elizabeth of York and their marriage united the two rival houses. The House of Tudor was represented by a red-and-white Tudor Rose.

A new Tudor king

Meet King Henry VIII! He is best known for marrying six times and changing the country's religion, but there is much more to Henry's reign, including battles, banquets, and beheadings.

Henry consumed over 5,000 calories a day—twice the amount of the average man.

Quest for a son

Henry was a family man of his time. His obsession with having a male heir led him to have six wives. Being a wife of Henry was dangerous and often ended badly.

Party time

Entertaining was a big part of Henry's court. This meant lots of lavish parties, feasts, and tournaments took place. The royal kitchen was kept busy making rich, exotic meals such as porpoise, seal, and roast goat, along with custard, gelatin, and cream.

Close advisors

Henry liked being in charge of an entire kingdom. But with great power came great responsibility. Henry needed some help running the country, so he appointed several advisors. Just like his wives, some of them didn't last very long.

Henry practiced his battlefield skills in jousts and tournaments, and owned several suits of armor.

Warrior king

Henry liked to think of himself as a king who could lead an army into battle. Luckily, the Tudor period was rampant with conflicts, and he was more than happy to join in with wars against France. He also built a brand new navy.

Hans Holbein the Younger was a German-Swiss Renaissance artist who painted portraits of English nobles, including Henry VIII and his queens.

A new era

Henry ruled over a new era called the Renaissance. This was an artistic movement that began in Europe. It was a time of new ideas in art, music, and literature. As a musician and poet himself, Henry was known as the "Renaissance Prince."

At the start of Henry's reign, there were many Catholic monasteries in England run by monks and nuns.

Religion in England

England was a Catholic country when Henry became king. The Pope was the head of the Church, but he wouldn't always do what Henry wanted. Henry's solution was to remove Catholicism and create the Church of England.

Henry's family

In 1485, a new family of rulers seized the English crown—the Tudors. After beating Richard III at the Battle of Bosworth Field, Henry VII's first concern as king was to help England become strong once more.

The first Tudor king

England had been left a much poorer country after years of civil war. To help raise money, Henry VII decided to increase taxes. The people did not like having to pay more money to the king, but England did start to grow under Henry's rule.

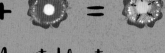

A united front

By marrying Elizabeth of York, Henry united the houses of York and Lancaster, who were responsible for the Wars of the Roses. To mark this union, Henry VII combined the white rose of York with the red rose of Lancaster to make the Tudor Rose.

Elizabeth of York

Henry VII

Arthur, Prince of Wales

Margaret Tudor, Queen of Scotland

Tudor tots

Henry VII wanted a son because having a male heir to the throne was the only way of keeping the Tudor line secure. Luckily, Elizabeth had two boys, Arthur and Henry. They also had two daughters, Mary and Margaret who later became queens of France and Scotland respectively.

Henry VIII

Mary Tudor, Queen of France

Tudor society

In Tudor society, people were ranked according to wealth. The king ruled over almost every aspect of life. Under the king were his nobles who were given land in return for their loyalty. Below them were lower-ranking landowners called gentry, and wealthy merchants. Next, were farmers. At the very bottom of society were servants, craftspeople, laborers, and the unemployed.

King

Nobles

Gentry and merchants

Farmers

Servants, craftspeople, laborers, and the unemployed

Royal duties

As king, Henry was expected to carry out a long list of duties, including:

Produce male children as heirs to the throne.

Prevent rebellion and law-breaking.

Defend the Church and worship God.

Lead his army and defend the country from foreign invasion.

Help his people live peaceful and successful lives.

Young Prince Henry

Prince Henry was not the heir to the throne, because he had an older brother, Arthur. While Arthur was being taught how to be a king, Henry could enjoy a more carefree childhood. On the grounds of Eltham Palace, he hunted, played sports, and learned languages, music, and poetry.

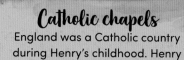

Catholic chapels

England was a Catholic country during Henry's childhood. Henry would attend church every day in his family's private chapel at Eltham Palace.

Outdoor fun

Henry could never be still or quiet for too long. He spent hours practicing archery, hunting, and horseback riding. He rode so much that he could tire out 12 horses in one afternoon! You might say that Henry's first love was sports.

Game, set, match

Before the game of tennis we know today, there was a sport called royal tennis. This was played on an indoor court, with a central net and high walls to bounce the ball off. It was one of Henry's favorite activities.

Master linguist

A son of a king wouldn't just speak one language. At a young age, Henry became fluent in three other languages alongside English: French, Spanish, and Latin. This meant he could read the Bible, which was written in Latin.

Musical star

Prince Henry loved music and had a true talent for it. He played the keyboard and recorder, he sang, and he even composed his own songs. Music would become a regular feature of Henry's court.

Bookworm

Henry's childhood wasn't all fun and games. As a prince of the Renaissance period, he was expected to be well-educated. Henry loved to read and even wrote his own poetry.

Award-winner

By age three, Henry held many royal titles, such as Duke of York. He was also made a Knight of the Bath. Being knighted was a special honor, which came with a strict code of conduct. Knights were required to be honorable, honest, and gentlemanly.

Becoming king

Prince Arthur's death in 1502 changed the course of Henry's life. Henry was now heir to the throne. He did not have long to wait, because in 1509 his father Henry VII died. At just 17 years old, Henry was crowned king of England.

Royal marriage

A few days before his Coronation, Henry married Katherine of Aragon. Royal marriages had two main aims. The first was to produce a male heir. The second was to form foreign partnerships. Katherine was the daughter of Isabella and Ferdinand, the rulers of Spain. Her marriage to Henry ensured that England and Spain would be allies.

Katherine was married to Prince Arthur first. Then he died and she married Henry.

Street celebrations

The crowd outside Westminster Abbey cheered as King Henry VIII and Queen Katherine left the church. To mark the special occasion, thousands of people lined the streets of London, which were decorated with gold cloth and tapestries. Parties were held all over England.

The big day

King Henry VIII's Coronation took place on June 24, 1509. Following tradition, Henry was crowned in a grand ceremony at Westminster Abbey. He swore the Coronation Oath, then a heavy crown covered with precious stones was placed on his head. Bells, drums, and trumpets signaled the start of his reign.

Fit for a king

For the Coronation, Henry wore a gold doublet (a tight-fitting jacket) embroidered with precious stones, and a crimson robe with fur. Over this, he slung a ruby baldric (a belt that carried a sword) across his shoulder.

Henry's crown was later used at the coronations of each of his children.

Katherine wore a gown of white satin and fur to the Coronation.

The royal court

Henry's reign was a time for new beginnings, and it was full of optimism and excitement. The King was happy to hand the day-to-day running of his kingdom over to his new advisors. This left him free to hunt, joust, and eat with the people at his court.

Top team

Henry VII's advisors had all been powerful nobles, but Henry VIII wanted to pick men from ordinary backgrounds. His main advisor was Cardinal Thomas Wolsey, the son of a butcher. Wolsey did everything he could to give Henry what he wanted.

Corrupt advisors

Henry's rule began with a bang. He arrested his father's advisors, Richard Empson and Edmund Dudley, and had the two men executed. This made Henry very popular with his people because Empson and Dudley were known for being dishonest and corrupt.

Henry later made Wolsey Lord Chancellor, which meant he was the most powerful minister in the country.

Royal residences

Henry had many castles and palaces, which included Greenwich Palace, Whitehall Palace, Windsor Castle, and the Tower of London. Like the monarchs before him, Henry spent the night before his Coronation in the Tower of London.

Greenwich Palace

Windsor Castle

On the road

Henry had 60 homes that he traveled between, and each time he did, hundreds of his courtiers joined him. Moving around the country meant Henry could visit different areas and keep in touch with his people, get out of London during the summer, and allow for his homes to be cleaned.

Henry's army

Henry grew up hearing stories of foreign wars fought by famous English kings. Edward III and Henry V had led England to glory against its enemy, France. Henry wanted to prove he was a warrior king capable of the same battlefield victories. In 1513, Henry set sail to invade France.

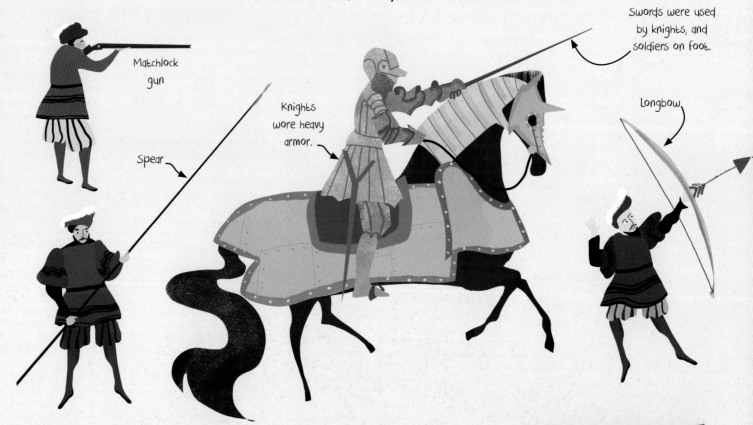

Matchlock gun

Swords were used by knights, and soldiers on foot.

Knights wore heavy armor.

Spear

Longbow

Tudor warfare

When Henry came to power, wars were fought by knights on horseback and soldiers on foot (called infantry) armed with longbows, spears, swords, and pikes. But during Henry's reign, firearms became popular. Matchlock guns and pistols brought new firepower to the battlefield.

Cannon

The road to war

Henry arrived in Calais, France, to lead an army of 25,000 soldiers to war. Even then, Henry traveled in style. His bed was set up in a gold pavilion, which was surrounded by 11 other tents, including one for his cook. Fourteen assistants, alongside 300 soldiers who were tasked with protecting him, escorted Henry wherever he went.

The superpowers of Europe

European nations were often at war with one another during the Tudor period. The three superpowers at that time were France, the Holy Roman Empire, and Spain. In 1511, the Holy Roman Empire and Spain declared war on France, and Henry joined in.

France   Holy Roman   Spain
            Empire

⚔ Battle of the Spurs

Henry's army surrounded the French town of Thérouanne and fired cannons at its walls. Then the English soldiers chased away the French knights, who left quickly. The knights used the spurs on their shoes to dig into their horses and get them to flee. That's why the battle became known as the "Battle of the Spurs."

Thérouanne

France

⚔ Battle of Flodden

While Henry battled with the French, Scotland had joined forces with France to invade England. Scotland launched an attack on Northumberland first. Queen Katherine sent an army in defense, which defeated the Scots at the Battle of Flodden.

Peace at last

In 1518, Thomas Wolsey organized a peace treaty (agreement) between England and the other European countries at war with France. They agreed not to attack one another. This treaty increased England's position in the world.

Fabulous festivals

It was a serious job being king, but no one knew how to party harder than Henry. Festivals were held regularly during his reign. Hundreds of guests gathered to enjoy music, tournaments, and games.

The Field of Cloth of Gold

In 1520, to mark the peace between France and England, Henry VIII and the French king, Francis I, held an 18-day festival. It was named after the gold cloth that covered their tents and costumes.

Food for the festival

Henry brought an army of cooks, which included 12 pastry chefs, 12 brewers, and 12 bakers. Huge cauldrons and a brick bread oven were used to prepare feasts that featured swan, eel, and even dolphin.

The portable palace was built from timber (wood) and covered with canvas that was painted to look like stone.

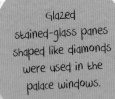

Glazed stained-glass panes shaped like diamonds were used in the palace windows.

A fountain that ran with wine stood in front of Henry's palace.

Inside the palace were bedrooms, a dining room, a chapel, and a courtyard.

The portable palace

It took 6,000 men three months to build Henry's portable palace for the festival. It was so grand that many people believed it was in fact a real palace!

Terrific tournaments

A party would not be complete without games. Tournaments were like pretend battles that mostly consisted of jousting and fighting on foot. Knights used these events to compete with each other.

Ready, set, joust

During a joust, two knights on horseback attempted to break their lances (long sticks) on their opponents' armor. Henry was a good jouster and once struck his opponent's armor so hard that sparks flew off.

Fight with Francis

Thomas Wolsey tried to make sure that Henry VIII and Francis I did not compete against each other during the festival. But Henry did not listen and challenged Francis to a wrestling match, which he lost!

On the last day of the festival there was a firework display, which may have included a rocket shaped like a dragon.

The day in numbers

An estimated **5,172** English guests attended the festival.

It cost Henry **£15,000** (around **$5.7 million** in today's money) to pay off his portion of the costs.

Henry's food supplies included **17 deer, 700 conger eels, 800 calves**, and **2,200 sheep**.

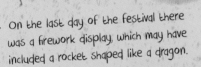

Henry's big problem

By 1526, Henry faced a dilemma. He had been married to Katherine for nearly 20 years, but she had not given him a male heir. Then, a young woman named Anne Boleyn caught his eye.

Henry wrote Anne many love letters in French. One promised Anne that: "Henceforth my heart shall be dedicated to you alone."

A new love

Anne Boleyn and Henry's romance began while she was working as Queen Katherine's helper. Anne came from a powerful family, and she could dance, sing, write poetry, and hunt. Henry fell in love with Anne and wanted to marry her.

No to divorce

In the 1500s, divorce was forbidden by the Catholic Church. To break up with Katherine, Henry would need special permission from Pope Clement VII. But Clement said no. What would Henry do now?

Henry was obsessed with having a male heir. He wanted to protect the Tudor dynasty, and it was feared that a female monarch could be easily overthrown.

A daughter, but no son

In 1516, Katherine had given birth to a daughter, Mary. Desperate for a son and convinced that Katherine would not give him one, Henry believed that his only option was to leave her.

Pope Clement VII

Route to divorce

Divorcing Katherine so Henry could marry Anne and, hopefully, secure a male heir wouldn't be easy. Henry went to great lengths to make it happen.

1 Henry ordered Wolsey to find a way of ending his marriage to Katherine. When Wolsey failed to do this, Henry accused him of betraying his country and arrested him for treason. Wolsey died not long before he was due to be executed.

4 Henry and his new advisors, Thomas Cranmer and Thomas Cromwell, worked on a cunning plan to resolve the King's problem. But what would they come up with?

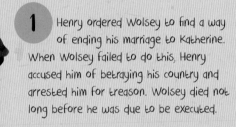

2 With Wolsey gone, Henry made Thomas More his Lord Chancellor. But More was a devout Catholic and refused to go against the Pope. He would not sign a document ending Henry's marriage.

Henry's new home

To apologize for failing to get him a divorce, Wolsey gifted the King Hampton Court Palace. But this gesture did not convince Henry to forgive him.

3 Anne refused to be Henry's mistress and said she would wait to become his wife. Henry moved Anne into Greenwich Palace. Katherine was furious at the news.

A new church

In 1533, Henry made a shocking announcement. He was cutting ties with the Catholic Church. In its place, he would create a new Church of England. This meant he no longer needed the Pope's permission to marry Anne Boleyn.

The Supreme Head

Henry asked Parliament to pass a law called "The Act of Supremacy." This made Henry the Supreme Head of the Church of England and confirmed the country's split from the Catholic Church. It gave Henry control over every aspect of England's religion.

The new archbishop

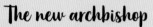

As one of Henry's advisors, Thomas Cranmer had helped plan the new Church of England. Henry then made him the Archbishop of Canterbury, which was the top religious job in the country.

Rise to fame

The idea to break ties with the Pope came from Thomas Cromwell. This plan led Henry to reward him generously. With Wolsey gone, Cromwell stepped into his shoes as Henry's main advisor.

Church of England

A not so happy ending

Finally, Henry ended his marriage to Katherine, and in 1533, he married Anne, who was pregnant with his child. But disappointing news followed, as Anne gave birth to a girl, and not a boy. They named her Elizabeth.

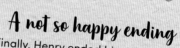

Closed for business

Now that England had split from the Catholic Church, Henry ordered the country's many Catholic monasteries to be closed. Their land and money was also taken and given to the King.

Up in flames

Cromwell ordered many Catholic relics to be collected and burned. These were special items of worship such as bones that Catholics believed belonged to dead saints.

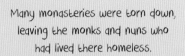

SOLD

Many monasteries were torn down, leaving the monks and nuns who had lived there homeless.

Henry's new Church of England began the period called the English Reformation.

Religion and people

For centuries, the Catholic Church had played a vital role in people's lives. However, some Catholic priests were seen as corrupt men who stole worshippers' money. Still, many Catholics were not happy with Henry's new church.

A new era

Henry's move away from the Catholic Church was not new. From around 1517, a religious revolution called the Reformation had been taking place in parts of Europe. This saw Catholicism replaced by a different branch of Christianity called Protestantism.

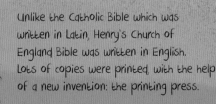

Unlike the Catholic Bible which was written in Latin, Henry's Church of England Bible was written in English. Lots of copies were printed, with the help of a new invention: the printing press.

Crime and punishment

Not everyone was happy with Henry's new Church of England, but those who disagreed with him were punished. This marked the beginning of King Henry's reign of terror.

Goodbye Anne

In 1536, Thomas Cromwell brought Henry some shocking news. He accused Anne of being unfaithful to him. Henry had her sent to the Tower of London, where she was executed. But the charges against Anne were probably lies made up by Cromwell, who hated her.

Ax or sword?

Executions were traditionally carried out by ax. For Anne's execution, Henry had a skilled swordsman brought over from France.

The end of More

Thomas More was another member of Henry's inner circle to suffer the King's anger. More refused to recognize Henry as the head of the Church, in place of the Pope. He was charged with treason and executed on July 1, 1535.

A warning to all

The Traitors' Gate was the entrance at the Tower of London used for prisoners charged with treason and sentenced to death. Their heads were often later displayed on pikes on London Bridge.

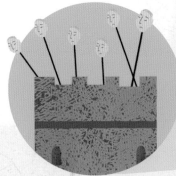

The Catholics revolt

Many people wanted England to remain a Catholic country. This led to major rebellions. In the north of England, more than 30,000 protestors marched to take over the city of York, in what was called the "Pilgrimage of Grace." Henry tricked the rebels into negotiating peace, but when the protest was over, he had them executed.

Sneaky spycraft

Henry developed unique methods for finding out who he could trust. He had watching wooden heads carved in the eaves (roof) of Hampton Court Palace to remind the people at his court that he had eyes and ears everywhere. This is where the term "eavesdropping" comes from.

A wall of wives

Although his previous marriages had ended in disaster, Henry was not done looking for a wife. After all, he still needed a male heir. Then, in 1536, Henry married Jane Seymour. But Jane would not be Henry's last wife.

The heir

On October 12, 1537 Henry's dream of having a male heir came true. Edward was next in line to the Tudor throne, ahead of his sisters.

Divorced

Katherine of Aragon

Beheaded

Anne Boleyn

Died

Jane Seymour

Jane Seymour had been a lady-in-waiting, or assistant, to Henry's first two wives—just like Anne Boleyn had been to Katherine of Aragon. Jane married Henry 11 days after Anne's execution, but she died shortly after giving birth to a son, Edward. Henry finally had his heir.

Divorced

Anne of Cleves

After Jane's death, Thomas Cromwell said he'd found Henry a new wife—a German princess named Anne of Cleves. But when Anne arrived in England, Henry claimed that she looked nothing like the portrait Cromwell had shown him. Henry ended the marriage after a few months.

Cromwell executed

Henry was furious with Cromwell for introducing him to Anne of Cleves. Henry charged him with treason and sent him to the Tower of London. Cromwell was executed in 1540.

Catherine Howard was the niece of the Duke of Norfolk, an advisor to Henry, who was later sentenced to death for treason.

Katherine Parr was more of a nurse to Henry than a wife who would give him more children.

Beheaded

Survived

Catherine Howard

A cousin of Anne Boleyn's, Catherine Howard married Henry in 1540. Although Henry called her "his rose without a thorn," he soon discovered that Catherine had been unfaithful to him. As with her cousin, Henry had Catherine executed.

Katherine Parr

Henry wasn't done yet! In 1543, Henry married his last wife, Katherine Parr. As Henry's health declined, Katherine made sure that he was well taken care of, and she was like a mother to his three children.

Military might

As Henry grew older, he worried about his place in history. Would future generations remember him as one of the great warrior kings of old? He decided he needed more military glory on the battlefield.

Each fort bore Henry's coat of arms, carved over the entrance.

The forts were a circular shape so that cannons could fire at enemy ships in any direction.

The Mary Rose was Henry VIII's favorite ship.

The gunports were opened for battle and closed in heavy seas.

Large cannons fired iron and stone balls through hinged flaps, called gunports.

Forts

Henry wanted to protect English shores by building fortresses along its coast. The forts, called "device forts," were built with the money and stone that were taken from the monasteries.

Navy

To fight with France and Scotland, Henry ordered a new fleet of navy warships to be built. Each ship carried around 185 soldiers and 30 gunners. After cannons fired at an enemy ship, the soldiers would board it and fight hand-to-hand.

The Rough Wooing

Henry suggested his son Edward marry Mary, Queen of Scots. When Scotland rejected this, Henry sent his army to change their minds. The English attacks on Scotland were known as the "Rough Wooing." But Henry's campaign did not work. Scotland joined forces with France, which sent its navy to attack England.

War again

Now that Henry had built up his navy and his forts, he felt better prepared for war. And soon he would declare war on France and Scotland. He turned to Scotland first, a country he was interested in controlling...

The *Mary Rose* took in water through its open gunports, and sank.

Battle of the Solent

In 1545, more than 200 French warships gathered near the Isle of Wight to invade England. However, Henry's flagship the *Mary Rose* led the English fleet out to meet them. Watching from the shore was Henry himself. But his excitement turned to dismay when the *Mary Rose* suddenly sank. Despite this terrible blow, Henry's navy was able to repel the French attack.

Dressed to kill

Henry's last suit of armor was supposed to show him as a dashing, crusading king. But it was a long way from the armor the young Henry had worn at the Field of Cloth of Gold festival. Now middle-aged, Henry was overweight and no longer fit to fight in battle.

Money worries

Henry's war against France and Scotland was a financial disaster. It would have cost billions in today's money. To pay for it, Henry demanded a new tax from landowners. Those who refused to pay were sent to the Tower of London.

To try and save some money, Henry made coins with a cheaper metal instead of silver and gold.

Henry's last days

By the mid 1540s, Henry was no longer the young, athletic king who had taken the throne. He was overweight, unwell, and unable to walk without the help of a wheelchair. He ruled England hidden away in the rooms of Whitehall Palace.

Walking wounded

In an earlier jousting accident Henry suffered an injury to his legs, which had never properly healed. He had painful wounds that smelled bad and made walking virtually impossible.

Wheel walker

By his mid-50s, Henry was very overweight. He also had such problems walking that he was pushed around in specially made wheelchairs called trams. He also used a pulley system to lift him up and down the stairs.

Final farewell

Henry grew very sick. It was treason to suggest that the King was dying, so no one wanted to tell Henry that death was near. Finally, Henry's close advisor, Anthony Denny, told Henry that he didn't have long to live and asked if he wanted to speak to Archbishop Cranmer. The conversation with Denny would be the King's last.

Last will

It was important for a king to make plans for after his death. Henry's will stated that Edward would become king. It also confirmed that if Edward died without an heir, his sisters Mary and then Elizabeth could be crowned queen.

Henry's remains are buried below a marble slab in the floor of St. George's Chapel at Windsor Castle.

The King is dead! Long live the King.

The end of an era

On January 28, 1547, King Henry VIII died, aged 55. A wax statue of the King was put on top of his coffin. The statue was draped in velvet and had a satin cap covered with jewels and gloves with rings over the fingers. The coffin was then placed on a carriage and taken through London to Windsor Castle.

Thousands of people on horseback and on foot lined the streets to mourn the loss of their king.

After Henry

During his almost 38-year reign, Henry changed England's religion, married six times, and went to war. Most of his decisions were led by his desire to have a son. But, in the end, it was Henry's daughters that ensured the Tudor line continued.

Mary I
1553–1558

Known as "Bloody Mary," Mary wanted to restore Catholicism to England and killed hundreds of Protestants in the process. She died of influenza in 1558.

Elizabeth did not have any children of her own, so the Tudor line ended with her. But a new branch of the royal family ruled instead.

Edward VI
1547–1553

After Henry died, his nine-year-old son Edward became king. Because of his young age, the country was controlled by a group of people who made all the decisions until Edward would be old enough to make them for himself. But Edward died at age 15.

Lady Jane Grey
1553

Lady Jane Grey was Edward's cousin. She was declared queen in place of the actual heir Mary. However, Mary took the throne nine days later and Jane was executed.

Elizabeth I
1558–1603

Elizabeth is remembered as one of the greatest monarchs in English history. Despite Mary's efforts, Elizabeth made her father's Church of England the country's main religion. She ruled over a "golden age," where England became very rich and powerful. Her father would have been proud.